Great Native Americans

Peter F. Copeland

DOVER PUBLICATIONS, INC.
Mineola, New York

Copyright

Copyright © 1997 by Dover Publications, Inc.
All rights reserved under Pan American and International Copyright Conventions.

Published in Canada by General Publishing Company, Ltd., 30 Lesmill Road, Don Mills, Toronto, Ontario.
Published in the United Kingdom by Constable and Company, Ltd., 3 The Lanchesters, 162–164 Fulham Palace Road, London W6 9ER.

Bibliographical Note

Great Native Americans is a new work, first published by Dover Publications, Inc., in 1997.

DOVER *Pictorial Archive* SERIES

This book belongs to the Dover Pictorial Archive Series. You may use the designs and illustrations for graphics and crafts applications, free and without special permission, provided that you include no more than four in the same publication or project. (For permission for additional use, please write to: Permissions Department, Dover Publications, Inc., 31 East 2nd Street, Mineola, N.Y. 11501.)
However, republication or reproduction of any illustration by any other graphic service, whether it be in a book or in any other design resource, is strictly prohibited.

International Standard Book Number: 0-486-29607-5

Manufactured in the United States of America
Dover Publications, Inc., 31 East 2nd Street, Mineola, N.Y. 11501

Introduction

The Native Americans have lived in North America since long before the first colonists came over from Europe, and from the start they have played a significant role in the history of the United States. Native Americans have acted as guides and teachers, as allies and as opponents in war, and as artists, educators and leaders of their people.

This book presents my portraits—based on authentic likenesses—of over 40 notable Native Americans who lived between the 16th and 20th centuries, with accompanying biographical sketches that highlight some of the most important episodes in each subject's life. It is not a complete list by any means; some important figures are omitted solely because no historic portrait is known to exist.

The stories of the war chiefs of the Indian tribes of North America—some of whom are featured in these pages—make for sad reading. These men and women fought for a losing cause against a remorseless and ever-advancing foe, who refused to allow the indigenous peoples to remain on their ancestral homelands, to recognize Native American culture as being of any importance, or to respect the Indian people as fellow human beings.

Peter F. Copeland

In 1754 **Queen Allaquippa** of the Delaware people met with George Washington, a young officer in Virginia's colonial militia, at a Delaware village in western Pennsylvania. At that time England and France were both seeking to expand their territories in America, and Washington was commissioned to bring gifts from the English in an attempt to keep the Delaware from allying with the French. Although Allaquippa accepted his offerings and promised her tribe's assistance, this and other similar trips proved largely unsuccessful; in the war that finally sprang up between the two nations, the English generals treated their native allies with contempt and therefore lost much of their support.

Born around 1820 in Arizona, **Barboncito** was a chief of the Navajo people when he signed the Doniphan Treaty of 1846, promising peace between the Navajo and the whites. Despite this agreement, the Navajo were forcibly removed from their land during the Civil War and relocated to Fort Sumner, New Mexico. Barboncito was the last Navajo leader to surrender to the whites; he eventually escaped from captivity, only to be recaptured.

Conditions in the new settlement were terrible, the land arid and unsuitable for farming. In 1868 Barboncito and other tribal headmen traveled to Washington to tell the President of their plight; the treaty that came from this meeting allowed the Navajo to return to a portion of their ancestral homeland, where they remain to this day.

Barboncito died in 1871, still a chief among his people, respected by whites and Indians alike.

Black Hawk, chief of the Sauk, was born in 1767 in northwestern Illinois, where he gained early fame for the expeditions he led against the Cherokee and Osage tribes. In the War of 1812 Black Hawk took sides with the British, after repudiating a treaty in which his people lost all their lands east of the Mississippi River. After the war, the defeated Black Hawk led his people back to the West, where he eventually tried to form a confederation of Indians against the white invaders; Black Hawk's War of 1832 resulted in a great slaughter of the tribes. Finally Black Hawk was imprisoned, during which time he wrote his autobiography, a classic account of white—Indian confrontations. He died in 1838 at the age of 71.

Blue Jacket was one of the Shawnee chiefs temporarily allied under Tecumseh. In 1790 Blue Jacket—accompanied by Little Turtle of the Miami—ambushed and defeated a mixed force of U. S. Army regulars and militiamen in Ohio. This action brought into that territory General Arthur St. Clair and 2,300 militiamen, who were themselves defeat-

ed, with more than 600 whites killed. These set-backs caused a temporary halt to white migration and prompted President Washington to raise a new militia under General Anthony Wayne. At the arrival of these forces, Little Turtle began to counsel peace, and he kept his Miami forces out of the disastrous Battle of Fallen Timbers (shown here), where Blue Jacket was defeated and forced to retreat. General Wayne followed, burning Indian villages as he advanced. In 1795 chiefs from twelve tribes, including Blue Jacket and Little Turtle, signed the Treaty of Greenville, setting up a definite boundary between Indian lands and white settle-ments and shattering Tecumseh's desired union.

A member of the Yankton Sioux, **Gertrude Simmons Bonnin** was one of a number of white-educated Native Americans who fought for fair treatment of her people by the federal government. She was born in 1876 in South Dakota and was educated both on the Sioux reservation and at schools in Indiana and Virginia. An author, reformer, orator and musician, she was also a teacher at the Carlisle Indian School in Pennsylvania and the composer of an Indian opera based upon the Plains Indians' Sun Dance. Her first book, *Old Indian Legends*, was published in 1901. Gertrude Simmons Bonnin died in 1938.

Billy Bowlegs was a Seminole chief who fought against U. S. troops in the Seminole War of 1835–1842. He was an ally of the Seminole leader Osceola and fought on after the latter's death and the surrender of many other Seminole chiefs. In 1842 Billy Bowlegs finally surrendered, although for more than a decade after that he resisted the relocation of his people from their Florida homeland to the Indian Territory in Oklahoma. At the outbreak of the Civil War, Billy Bowlegs and other chiefs sided with the Union and for a time held off the Confederates in a series of desperate battles; ultimately he and his men were forced to retreat to Kansas, where Billy Bowlegs eventually died.

11

Thayendanegea, known to the whites as **Joseph Brant**, was chief of the Mohawk tribe of the Iroquois Nation during both the French and Indian War and the American Revolution; in each of these conflicts he allied himself with the English. Born in 1742, Brant was a devout Christian, a missionary who had translated parts of the Bible into the Mohawk tongue, but he was also a fierce fighter, leading his warriors on many raids on American settlements in New York and Pennsylvania. After the Revolution, Joseph Brant arranged a land grant in Canada for his people, where they settled along the Grand River in Ontario. He died in 1807.

Cornplanter, a chief of the Seneca tribe in the Iroquois confederacy, was an ally of the French in the French and Indian War. Later, like his fellow Iroquois chief Joseph Brant, Cornplanter was to side with the English against the colonists during the Revolutionary War. When peace resumed, Cornplanter became a spokesman for the Seneca people, in 1790 entering into negotiations with the newly formed government in Philadelphia. In 1801 he visited President Thomas Jefferson in Washington, D.C., to discuss Seneca landholdings; his diplomatic efforts won his people a land grant in Pennsylvania. Cornplanter supported the American cause in the War of 1812; he died in 1836, at the age of 104.

Curly, born in 1859, was a Crow Indian scout in the U. S. Army during the wars against the Sioux. In June 1876 he was attached to General George Custer's cavalry detachment, which was looking for hostile Indians along the Rosebud River in Montana. Curly was wounded at the Battle of Little Bighorn, where Custer and his men were slaughtered by an alliance of Sioux and Cheyenne warriors. Curly managed to disguise himself as a Sioux and flee the field; two days later, he brought news of the battle to the Army supply ship "Far West." In later years Curly was involved in a dispute with the government over his retirement pay, a dispute which he won before his death in 1923. He is buried in the National Cemetery at the Custer Battlefield.

Born in 1871 on the Winnebago reservation in Nebraska, **Angel DeCora Dietz** was influential in the shaping of Indian art and affairs in the early years of the 20th century. She graduated from the Hampton Institute in 1891 and studied art at Smith College, the Drexel Institute and at the Boston Museum of Fine Arts. Busy as an artist and illustrator of books, Angel DeCora Dietz also spent much time lecturing on the problems confronting Native Americans. She became the head of the art department at the Carlisle Indian School and with her husband, the Sioux teacher William Dietz, became active in Indian affairs, eventually meeting with President Theodore Roosevelt to discuss the concerns of Native Americans. Angel DeCora Dietz died in the great flu epidemic of 1919.

As war chiefs of the Cheyenne, **Dull Knife** and **Little Wolf** earned their titles through prowess in battle, leading their warriors in resistance to the invasion of their western lands by the whites in the years following the Civil War. The cross worn on the breast of Dull Knife in this picture is not a religious symbol: for spiritual strength he carried the lizard charm shown at the bottom.

Four Bears was the second chief of the Mandan people in 1832 when the artist George Catlin visited the tribe and painted the portrait upon which this drawing is based. He led his people against many neighboring tribes in the 1830s and was selected as chief of the Mandans in 1837, the same year that a smallpox epidemic struck and nearly wiped out the Mandans altogether. Almost overnight the tribe was reduced from sixteen hundred to around thirty members; Four Bears was among the victims of the plague.

The most famous of Apache warriors, **Geronimo** came to symbolize the spirit of Native American resistance to the invasion of Indian lands by white settlers. Born in 1829, he became the foremost leader of his people in battles with both Mexican and U. S. forces in the last of the Apache wars, resisting all attempts to settle his people on reser- vations. After his surrender to the U. S. Army in 1886, Geronimo and hundreds of other Apaches were sent in chains to prisons in Florida and then relocated to Alabama and Oklahoma. Geronimo was never granted permission to return to the ancient Apache homelands before his death in 1909.

Hendrick was born at the end of the 17th century and elected chief of the Mohawk tribe while still a young man. He allied himself with the British and in 1710 visited England, where he was presented to Queen Anne as the "King of the Mohawks." As a friend of the British, Hendrick at age 70 went to war against the French; he was killed along with many of his men at the Battle of Lake George in 1755.

Chief **Joseph**, born in 1832 in what is now the state of Washington, became one of the great Indian military commanders of the 19th century. Spurred on by the discovery there of gold, whites had encroached upon the lands of the Nez Percé, ignoring Joseph's protestations that their presence was unlawful. Finally the dispute brought about the use of arms, and in 1877 Chief Joseph led his people into battle, wiping out a U. S. force at White Bird canyon. Eighteen more battles followed, with the Nez Percés continuing to prevail, until the arrival of superior U. S. forces prompted Chief Joseph to lead his people on a fighting retreat. They had covered over 1,500 miles, constantly pursued by the Army, before they surrendered near the Canadian border. Despite the promises of the opposing commanders, the defeated Nez Percés were sent to the Indian Territory in Oklahoma. Resolved to fight no more, Chief Joseph remained the spokesman for his tribe and visited Washington, D.C. several times before his death in 1904.

Born in the 1780s in Illinois, **Keokuk** became a chief of the Sauk as a reward for his bravery in battle against the Sioux. But many of Keokuk's people came to regard him as a traitor for capitulating with the American government in the division of Sauk lands; Black Hawk, the legitimate leader of the Sauk, defied the treaties that the other had made, leading his followers against Keokuk and the American forces in what would come to be known as Black Hawk's War. Keokuk died in 1848.

King Philip, whose Wampanoag Indian name was Metacomet, was given his nickname by the Plymouth settlers in Massachusetts. A son of the friendly sachem, Massasoit, he became a chief in 1662 at the age of 24. He led an alliance of Indian tribes against the colonists, believing that their presence would bring about the extermination of his people. The conflict that arose became known as King Philip's War, and it came close to wiping out the settlements in Massachusetts and Rhode Island. Eventually, however, the Indian confederation began to weaken, and by 1676 King Philip was defeated and many of his followers sold into slavery by the victorious colonists. Philip himself was killed, his head cut off and displayed in the Plymouth settlement.

The first female Indian physician, **Susan La Flesche** was born into the Sioux in 1865 and graduated from the Woman's Medical College of Pennsylvania. She administered to Native American tribes, traveling on horseback from her home in Omaha, Nebraska. Eventually La Flesche became a Presbyterian missionary, heading a delegation to the nation's capital to fight for the prohibition of liquor. She died at age 50 in 1915, having spent her life in the service of her people. The symbol depicted at the bottom of the picture represents an Indian goddess against disease.

Little Turtle, adopted into the Miami tribe, was born in 1752 in the Illinois country. As a war chief of the Miami tribe, he defeated U. S. General Josiah Harmar on the Miami River in 1791 and General Arthur St. Clair at St. Marys. Little Turtle initially fought alongside Blue Jacket, but by the time of the great Indian defeat at Fallen Timbers he had begun to counsel peace, and he did not fight in this battle. In 1797 he met George Washington and became an ally of the Americans. Little Turtle kept the Miamis neutral during Tecumseh's wars against the whites. He died at Fort Wayne, Indiana, in 1812.

Mangas Coloradas, whose name in Spanish means "Red Sleeves," became a chief of the Apaches in 1838, when he was almost fifty years old. He was described as "an athletic man, well over six feet in height, with . . . long hair that reached to his waist. . . . [He] presented quite a model of physical manhood." Mangas allied his people with the United States during the Mexican War of the 1840s, but incursions by the Americans into Apache lands later brought war with the U. S. Army and death to the Apache chief, who was killed by U. S. soldiers while being held a prisoner.

Maria Martínez and her husband Julian spent years studying and collecting the ancient art of pottery as practiced by the tribes of the Southwest, including her own Pueblo tribe, and they organized the Indian Village Exhibit at the St. Louis World's Fair in 1904. Maria Martínez began to use the ancient techniques in her own pottery making, perfecting the old method of applying the satiny black finish that became a hallmark of her art. Her pottery won her worldwide recognition, and she made many trips to exhibit her work throughout the United States and abroad. Maria and Julian Martínez had several children, all of whom have made a mark in the world of Native American art.

A Fox chief and the son of Chief Chimakassee, **Nesouaquoit** visited Washington, D.C., together with Keokuk and Black Hawk in 1833 to meet President Andrew Jackson. Nesouaquoit is seen here wearing an animal skin mantle symbolizing the Bear Clan, from which the Fox people choose their leaders.

Okeemaquid was a great warrior of the Ojibwa, or Chippewa, people in the early years of the 19th century, during their wars with the Sioux. The feathered headdress he wears was given him by a Sioux chief upon the declaration of peace between the two tribes in 1825. This present was in accordance with the Indian custom of giving gifts at peace parleys.

Osceola was born into the Creek tribe at the beginning of the 19th century and is thought to have fought against Andrew Jackson in the War of 1812 and again in 1818. For a time he served the government by policing the Seminole reservation in Florida, but his loyalties evaporated after the Treaty of Payne's Landing (1832) was signed, an agreement that would have the Indians moved west of the Mississippi. Osceola attained a position of leadership among the Seminole and led them into the Seminole War of 1835, harassing the white troops from the swamps where hc had hidden his people. In 1837 Osceola was captured and imprisoned at a peace conference while under a flag of truce; he died the following year.

Quanah Parker, the son of a white mother and a Comanche father, was born about 1845 in Texas. As a tribal leader he refused to accede to government demands that the Comanches remove themselves into the Indian Territory, and for much of the 1870s he made war on the frontier towns and white settlements in Texas. Although never truly defeated, Qua-nah Parker finally surrendered and settled in the Indian Territory, where he became a judge in the Court of Indian Affairs. In later years he traveled widely as a representative of his tribe, touring with the Apache chief Geronimo and other notable Native American personalities of the day.

When the Pawnee chief **Petalesharro** visited Washington, D.C., in 1821, a local newspaper reported that he had saved the life of a young woman who was fated to be sacrificed by his tribe; Petalesharro at once became a sensation, and indeed he is credited with ending the practice of human sacrifice among his people. Petalesharro signed the Pawnee Treaty of 1825 and is thought by some to have died in the 1830s, when his people were decimated by an outbreak of smallpox; others believe that he was still alive to sign a treaty in 1857 as "Petanesharo, the man and the chief."

1616

Pocahontas, whose Indian name was Matoaka, was probably born into the Pamunkey tribe between 1595 and 1597. Pocahontas was the favorite daughter of Powhatan, chief of the Virginia Confederacy of Tribes. It is thought that she pleaded for and saved the life of Captain John Smith of Jamestown, who had been captured by her father's warriors and sentenced to death. She is also credited with bringing food to the people of Jamestown at times when they were near starvation. Pocahontas eventually converted to Christianity and married an English planter, who brought her to England, where she died in 1617.

Pontiac led a confederation of Indian tribes (including his Ottawa people) against the British at the end of the French and Indian War. Whereas the French had maintained good relations with these tribes, the British had been far less friendly to and respectful of the Indians; when the British began to invade Indian hunting grounds, Pontiac mobilized the tribes and set ablaze frontier settlements in Pennsylvania, Maryland and Virginia. Although the rebellion was undertaken by a greater alliance of Indians than had been formed ever before or since, in 1763 Pontiac was forced to sue for peace. He was murdered in 1769, perhaps by an Indian in the pay of the English.

Powhatan, the father of Pocahontas, was the first Native American leader to have any important contact with the first European colonists in North America. Nearly 60 years old when the colonists arrived, Powhatan was chief of the Powhatan Confederacy, comprised of thirty tribes whose territory stretched from the Potomac River to Albermarle Sound in North Carolina. Athough Powhatan had maintained peace with the English settlers at Jamestown, his death in 1618 saw the beginning of strife and warfare between the two groups. This drawing of Powhatan is from the only known portrait of the chief, drawn by a 17th-century European artist.

A Hunkpapa Sioux war chief, **Rain-in-the-Face** was born in 1835 in the Dakota territory. Rain-in-the-Face was a leader in the Sioux resistance to the whites in the 1860s, and he joined with Sitting Bull and his Sioux and Cheyenne warriors to participate in the Battle of Little Bighorn in 1876; some say that it was he who killed General Custer. Rain-in-the-Face followed Sitting Bull on his retreat into Canada and later, returning south, surrendered at Fort Keogh, Montana. He died in North Dakota in 1905 at age 70.

Red Cloud was born in Nebraska in 1822, a member of the Oglala Sioux tribe, and as tribal chief he led his people in several important victories over the U. S. Army. Red Cloud fiercely opposed the westward movement of the white settlers and in 1866, with Rain-in-the-Face, destroyed a detachment of troops under Captain William Fetterman in what was to be known as the "Fetterman Massacre." For a time Red Cloud nearly succeeded in halting all western migration into Indian lands, until he saw that continued resistance was useless and that the whites were too many to oppose. Red Cloud counseled peace to Sitting Bull and Crazy Horse during the troubles that led up to the Custer massacre in 1876. He was eventually removed as chief and forced to live on the Pine Ridge Reservation where, blind and ailing, he died in 1909.

Red Jacket, chief of the Seneca, was born around 1751 near Geneva, New York. Named for the jacket he received from the British during the Revolution, he later urged his people to ally themselves with the Americans, whom they joined in the War of 1812. Red Jacket was concerned, however, with the loss of his people's traditions, and throughout his life he fought to preserve the old customs, to little or no avail. Shown here with the medal of friendship he received from George Washington, Red Jacket continued to lead his people until 1821, when he was deposed in part due to his increasing dependence upon alcohol. He died in 1830, leaving two wives and seventeen children.

Satanta, the "Orator of the Plains," was a Kiowa chief. He was born around 1830 and was one of the leaders to sign the Medicine Lodge Treaty of 1867, in which his tribe agreed to go on a reservation. Famed as both a warrior and as an eloquent speaker in tribal councils and treaty negotiations, Satanta was arrested in 1871 for leading a raid on a wagon train. Satanta was initially freed and then again imprisoned, and he committed suicide in 1878 by jumping out of a hospital window in Huntsville, Texas.

Sequoyah was born in Tennessee during the 1760s or 1770s, his father probably a white trader named Nathaniel Gist and his mother a Cherokee. Sequoyah was an outstanding silversmith and, more importantly, the inventor of the Cherokee alphabet. His invention was at first regarded with scorn and suspicion, but soon the idea caught on; within a matter of months thousands of Cherokees had taught themselves to read and write in their own language. Sequoyah died in Mexico in 1843 while searching for a lost Cherokee tribe believed to have settled there before the Revolution. He is shown here holding a tablet on which the alphabet he devised is written.

Sitting Bull is the best remembered of the Sioux and Cheyenne leaders who fought the U. S. Army in the last great organized resistance to white domination of the plains of the Dakotas and Montana. Along with the Sioux chiefs Crazy Horse, Gall, Crow King, Hump and Fast Bull, Sitting Bull confronted General George Custer and the 7th Cavalry regi- ment at Little Bighorn; in less than one half hour the general and the more than 200 men of his regi- ment were killed. Sitting Bull was a dynamic leader and one of the most able in Native American histo- ry. He was killed by members of the Indian Police in 1890.

Kidnapped by whites as a young man and sold into slavery in Spain, **Squanto** managed to escape from bondage and return to his people. He befriended the settlers at the Plymouth settlement in Massachusetts (who shortened his full name of Tisquantum to its now-familiar form) and taught them to plant corn, arranging as well a treaty between them and the local Indians that remained unbroken for fifty years. Squanto performed many other acts of friendship for the English colonists before he died in 1622 of "Indian fever."

As a young man the Shawnee chief **Tecumseh** was taught to read and write in English, and from his subsequent reading he came to believe that the whites had no moral right to invade the land which had historically been free to all men, nor any right to erect fences and drive the Indians off the land. He became a preacher and a leader in the cause of unifying all of the tribes into one great confederacy that would oppose settlement by whites. When this came to the attention of the government, William Henry Harrison, then governor of the Indiana Territory, attacked the Shawnee at Tippecanoe, throwing the Indian union fatally off balance. The War of 1812 further disintegrated the confederacy, as members of the alliance took opposing sides in the conflict. Tecumseh sided with the British and died at the Battle of the Thames River in 1813; with him died the dream of a great Indian union.

Chief **Tiupanamabu** of the Nootka people of the Pacific Northwest is seen here carrying a harpoon as used by whale fishermen and wearing a fur mantle and a woven whaler's hat. His hat is decorated with depictions of hunters harpooning whales from canoes, the way of life of his seafaring people. It was a Nootka chief's prerogative to act as the harpooner on whale hunts.

Two Guns White Calf was born into the Blackfoot tribe in 1872. He became familiar to Americans in the early part of the 20th century when his picture appeared in newspapers across the country as a symbol of the "vanishing American." Two Guns White Calf was one of three Indians who posed for the Indian profile on the buffalo nickel designed by James Earle Fraser. He died of pneumonia in 1934.

Born in 1795 in the Dakotas, the chief **Waneta**—like so many other Sioux—initially resisted accepting the sovereignty of the newly formed American government, instead joining his father in supporting the British in the War of 1812. He later became an ally of the Americans, however, and signed both the Treaty of Fort Pierre and the Treaty of Prairie du Chien, which established the boundaries of the Sioux nation. Waneta died in 1848 in Beaver Creek, North Dakota.

Washakie was an eastern Shoshone, born in Utah about 1804 and made a chief in the 1840s. Washakie and his people maintained peaceful relations with the white settlers who crossed tribal lands on their way west, but they fought many battles with their traditional enemies the Sioux and Cheyenne, sometimes even allying themselves with the U. S. Army in these conflicts. When Washakie was about 70 years of age, some of the younger men in his tribe attempted to depose him as chief. Washakie left the camp, only to reappear at a council meeting two months later with six scalps he had taken, disproving the younger men's assertion that he was too old to maintain his chieftaincy. Washakie died and was buried with military honors in Montana at nearly one hundred years of age, still a chief among his people.

Born in northern California in 1842, **Winema** (better known as Toby Riddle) was an important figure in the Modoc War of 1872–73. She was already famed for her fearless exploits, having fought alongside the Modoc men in battle and once having killed a grizzly bear. By the time of the war, she had married a white man, Frank Riddle, and become alienated from many in her tribe. This estrangement grew when, serving as a translator for the Army, Winema revealed to Army commanders a Modoc plot to kill them when they met to arrange a peace: they ignored her warnings, however, and two of the three government representatives were killed at the meeting. Winema died in 1932.